John Winthrop

Politician and Statesman

Colonial Leaders

Lord Baltimore
English Politician and Colonist

Benjamin Banneker
American Mathematician and Astronomer

Sir William Berkeley
Governor of Virginia

William Bradford
Governor of Plymouth Colony

Jonathan Edwards
Colonial Religious Leader

Benjamin Franklin
American Statesman, Scientist, and Writer

Anne Hutchinson
Religious Leader

Cotton Mather
Author, Clergyman, and Scholar

Increase Mather
Clergyman and Scholar

James Oglethorpe
Humanitarian and Soldier

William Penn
Founder of Democracy

Sir Walter Raleigh
English Explorer and Author

Caesar Rodney
American Patriot

John Smith
English Explorer and Colonist

Miles Standish
Plymouth Colony Leader

Peter Stuyvesant
Dutch Military Leader

George Whitefield
Clergyman and Scholar

Roger Williams
Founder of Rhode Island

John Winthrop
Politician and Statesman

John Peter Zenger
Free Press Advocate

Revolutionary War Leaders

John Adams
Second U.S. President

Ethan Allen
Revolutionary Hero

Benedict Arnold
Traitor to the Cause

King George III
English Monarch

Nathanael Greene
Military Leader

Nathan Hale
Revolutionary Hero

Alexander Hamilton
First U.S. Secretary of the Treasury

John Hancock
President of the Continental Congress

Patrick Henry
American Statesman and Speaker

John Jay
First Chief Justice of the Supreme Court

Thomas Jefferson
Author of the Declaration of Independence

John Paul Jones
Father of the U.S. Navy

Lafayette
French Freedom Fighter

James Madison
Father of the Constitution

Francis Marion
The Swamp Fox

James Monroe
American Statesman

Thomas Paine
Political Writer

Paul Revere
American Patriot

Betsy Ross
American Patriot

George Washington
First U.S. President

Famous Figures of the Civil War Era

Jefferson Davis
Confederate President

Frederick Douglass
Abolitionist and Author

Ulysses S. Grant
Military Leader and President

Stonewall Jackson
Confederate General

Robert E. Lee
Confederate General

Abraham Lincoln
Civil War President

William Sherman
Union General

Harriet Beecher Stowe
Author of Uncle Tom's Cabin

Sojourner Truth
Abolitionist, Suffragist, and Preacher

Harriet Tubman
Leader of the Underground Railroad

Colonial Leaders

John
Winthrop

Politician and Statesman

Elizabeth Russell Connelly

Arthur M. Schlesinger, jr.
Senior Consulting Editor

Chelsea House Publishers

Philadelphia

Produced by Pre-Press Company, Inc., East Bridgewater, MA 02333

CHELSEA HOUSE PUBLISHERS
Editor in Chief Stephen Reginald
Production Manager Pamela Loos
Art Director Sara Davis
Director of Photography Judy L. Hasday
Managing Editor James D. Gallagher
Senior Production Editor J. Christopher Higgins

Staff for *JOHN WINTHROP*
Project Editor Anne Hill
Associate Art Director Takeshi Takahashi
Series Design Keith Trego

The Chelsea House World Wide Web address is http://www.chelseahouse.com

First Printing
1 3 5 7 9 8 6 4 2

Library of Congress Cataloging-in-Publication Data

Connelly, Elizabeth Russell.
    John Winthrop /Elizabeth Russell Connelly.
        p. cm. — (Colonial leaders)
    Includes bibliographical references (p.) and index.
    ISBN 0-7910-5965-0 (HC); 0-7910-6121-3 (PB)
    1. Winthrop, John, 1588–1649—Juvenile literature. 2. Governors—
Massachusetts—Biography—Juvenile literature. 3. Puritans—Massachusetts—
Biography—Juvenile literature. 4. Massachusetts—History—Colonial period,
ca. 1600–1775—Juvenile literature. 5. Puritans—Massachusetts—History—
17th century—Juvenile literature. [1. Winthrop, John, 1588–1649. 2. Governors.
3. Puritans. 4. Massachusetts—History—Colonial period, ca. 1600–1775.]
I. Title. II. Series.

F67.W79 C66 2000
974.4'02'092—dc21
[B]   00-038398

Acknowledgments: Thank you to Oona Beauchard
at the Massachusetts Historical Society

Publisher's Note: In Colonial and Revolutionary War America, there were no standard rules for spelling, punctuation, capitalization, or grammar. Some of the quotations that appear in the Colonial Leaders and Revolutionary War Leaders series come from original documents and letters written during this time in history. Original quotations reflect writing inconsistencies of the period.

Contents

The Winthrop family lived at Groton Hall, the family estate in Suffolk County in eastern England. John Winthrop's father, Adam, managed the estate for his older brother. The estate was large and included many farms, fields, orchards, and pastures.

A Young Gentleman

Amid gently rolling hills and fields of wheat and barley stood a simple manor. Sheep grazed not far from horse stables and a barn filled with cows and pigs. Sparkling stars reflected across ponds and a crescent moon cast shadows through the trees. This small estate in Edwardstone, a village in the English countryside, was the home of Adam and Anne Winthrop. On this cold winter night, Mr. Winthrop was pacing back and forth by the parlor fireplace. He was nervous because his wife was about to give birth. Then early the next morning, just before dawn, a baby cried out. It was January

22, 1588, and the Winthrops named their new-born son John.

John Winthrop was born into a wealthy family. But his ancestors hadn't always been well-to-do. John's grandfather had been born rather poor. But he worked very hard in the cloth trade and eventually earned enough money to open a store in London. That business was so successful that John's grandfather was able to buy a grand home with plenty of land around it. He found this home in Groton, a village near Edwardstone, in Suffolk County. Because of his new wealth, John's grandfather had finally risen to the rank of gentleman. And now that they owned a large estate, the Winthrops were considered part of the landed gentry.

When John's grandfather died, John's uncle (for whom John was named) inherited Groton Manor. But it was Adam, John's father, who actually managed the estate. He moved his family there when John was just four years old. Adam bought more property and improved the way the estate was farmed. The family fortune continued to grow. He also got involved in local government, which helped the Winthrops keep a respected position in the county. At the same time, Adam was training John to manage the family estate.

John was the only boy in his family. He had an older sister named Anne. His two younger sisters were Jane and Lucy. As the young son of a gentleman, John was given a proper education. He was taught spelling, grammar, history, and other subjects by a local Puritan minister. John learned to read in a household well stocked with Bibles and books about Puritan beliefs. Indeed, John's parents wanted him to learn to read so he could understand the Bible. On Sundays, the whole family would go to St. Bartholomew's Church in the morning and read the Bible in the afternoon. Sunday was a day of rest, so no one–parents or children–was allowed to work or play.

In 1602, when John was 14 years old, his father enrolled him at Trinity College, Cambridge.

Though entering college at 14 is young by today's standards, it was typical for the time. It was also typical for young men to study for a few years and then leave school without a degree. Often they needed to return home to manage the family property or business. John stayed at Trinity for about a year and a half and came home between semesters. He worked closely with his father to complete his training as lord of the estate. Sometime during his second year, he met a young woman named Mary Forth.

Mary was the only child of a Puritan family in nearby Stambridge. The Winthrops and the Forths were both wealthy landowners and shared the same religious beliefs. They wanted their children to marry well. The parents soon agreed that John and Mary would be a good match, so they encouraged their children's marriage. Thus, in April 1605, when he was just 17 years old, John married Mary Forth. They spent their two-week honeymoon in London. When the couple returned to Groton, they enjoyed a wedding feast with John's parents, aunts, uncle, and sisters.

The following year, after the birth of a son, John Jr., the young family moved to a small estate in Stambridge. The estate was part of Mary's **dowry**—a wedding gift from her family. John devoted himself to managing the land, while Mary tended to their home and growing family. Thanks to his father's early training, John was a great success at managing his estate. He turned a tidy profit from the land. In 1610, John bought Groton Manor from his uncle but John and Mary didn't move in right away. They stayed near her family in Stambridge for a while longer. Meanwhile, John's father continued to manage Groton.

When John and Mary finally left Stambridge, they moved their family into grand Groton Manor. John's father and mother remained in Groton Hall, a smaller home on the property. The huge estate provided for almost all of the needs of the growing Winthrop family and its workers. They made breads, sweets, and other foods in their bakehouse. They could store more than a year's supply of food in the enormous pantry. They raised horses, cattle, sheep, and pigs—some for eating, some for selling. They made their own beer in a special brewing-house. Local markets provided cloth, cooking pots, and other household items. With the estate running so smoothly, John decided to return to school. In 1613, he went to Gray's Inn in London to study law.

Unfortunately, soon thereafter, John had much to grieve. In June 1615, his wife Mary died. She was buried in the family tomb in Groton. In their 11 years together, John and Mary had had six children. Two daughters had died at birth. Their other four children were sons John Jr., Henry, Forth, and a daughter named Mary. John was almost 28 years old and his oldest child was only nine. It was difficult for him to raise the children by himself, so his mother and sisters helped out.

Gray's Inn is one of London's four Inns of Court, the buildings where students have gathered to learn to become lawyers since medieval times. Today, they are still an important part of the English legal system.

Six months later on December 6, John Winthrop married Thomasine Clopton, the daughter of a powerful and wealthy merchant family from Groton. But John and Thomasine never even celebrated their first wedding anniversary. Thomasine died giving birth to their first child. These few years were tragic times for John. Though his financial fortunes were growing, he suffered great personal loss.

Through it all, John began to take a more active role in the day-to-day running of the Groton estate. He spent time with his children, who were once again without a mother. For the second time in two years, John's mother also devoted more time to taking care of the children. In 1617, John was made a **justice of the peace** in Suffolk, which meant he would be away from home even more. In this new job, John's legal studies came in handy. He had to know the law well to settle disagreements between landlords and tenants and to deal with government officials. His family life also took a turn for the better.

John had been courting Margaret Tyndal and the two were very much in love. Margaret was a very attractive woman—intelligent, gracious, and beautiful. She was also a woman of great faith.

In March 1618, John and Margaret were married. John felt his third wife was his greatest treasure on earth. When he traveled away from home, he never failed to send her letters. John expressed deep love for Margaret in every letter. He also encouraged her faith. He believed that their first and greatest love must be for God, as they were very devout **Puritans.**

As lord of Groton Manor, John was head of the entire Winthrop family. He was now also a full member of the Suffolk gentry. But troubled times were coming. By the late 1620s, England was in the middle of a depression. John was very concerned with helping his three sons. They were ready to start their own careers at a very difficult time. Workers all over the country were out of jobs. Landowners like John were having trouble because of crop failures and difficulty selling what crops they could harvest. People couldn't afford to buy their livestock. Many people suffered severe poverty when they lost their jobs and homes. Others were dying of hunger and disease. John wrote in his journal that the streets were filled with people who looked like "wandering ghosts in the shape of men." He worried that those who had lost everything would turn to mugging, stealing horses, or even rioting. He didn't know how to help everyone, but he had to find a better way to support his own family.

John decided to take a second job. In 1627, he became an attorney at the Court of Wards and Liveries in London. Much of John's work came from **Parliament.** He was responsible for writing the bills that they might vote into law. John also had high hopes for a long and successful career in Parliament. But then in 1629, King Charles I dismissed Parliament and announced he would rule alone. The king raised taxes and generally made life very difficult for Puritans. He also put Parliament's Puritan leaders in prison. John thus gave up any hope of a parliamentary career. He was a strong Puritan and this king was very anti-Puritan. The king's policies pushed

Charles I of England (shown here with his wife, Henrietta) had many disagreements with the English Parliament over how the country should be governed.

John to the brink of despair. His only hope, he concluded, was to escape. He was 41 years old and married for the third time. He was concerned for the future of his many children and grandchildren. He prayed that God would provide them with "a shelter and a hiding place" elsewhere.

John Winthrop and the first group of
Massachusetts Bay Company colonists
sailed from England on the *Arbella* and 11
other ships on April 8, 1630, to establish a
Puritan settlement.

2

Architect for Massachusetts Bay

In 17th-century England, there was no such thing as freedom of religion. There was only the Church of England. Christians who didn't like the Church of England had two choices: they could either work to reform it from within, or leave it altogether. Those who wanted to break from the church were called Separatists. The Puritans were not Separatists. They were unhappy with the Church of England, but they didn't want to leave it completely. They wanted to purify it by working from within. That's why they came to be known as Puritans.

During this difficult time, a group of wealthy Puritans got together. They were worried about their country. They thought the government and church were corrupt. They felt their countrymen were too concerned with money and not concerned enough for the poor. In their view, if England didn't change its ways, it would be punished by God.

Some of these Puritans formed the Massachusetts Bay Company. In those days, groups of investors would put their money together and form trading companies. But to form a company, they needed the king's approval. The king decided who would get a charter to trade and establish a colony in America. Once the company was chartered, it would send workers to the New World to get furs, spices, and other exotic goods. The workers then shipped these goods back to England, where they were sold for a profit.

John's brother-in-law was a member of the Massachusetts Bay Company. Knowing John's concerns for his family, he encouraged John to

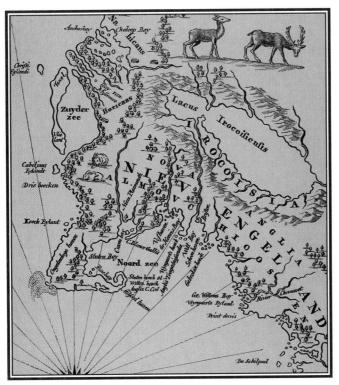

At the time that Massachusetts Bay Company colonists set sail for the New World, maps of the area were incomplete and inaccurate. This early Dutch map shows what explorers thought New England looked like. Cape Cod is in the lower left corner.

join the company. John discovered that many of his colleagues from the Court of Wards were also members. He was very interested in joining so he could practice his religion as he saw fit. He also wanted to get his family away from corrupt England. John was especially worried about his son, Henry, who had begun to rebel against his faith. John wondered if moving to a new land would be better for everyone. He wanted to worship God freely and raise his children as good Puritans. After giving it a lot of thought, John joined the company in 1629.

Over the next several months, John went to many meetings. Some of these meetings had to be held in secret because the Puritans were worried about being punished by the king. John and several others interviewed Puritans who wanted to settle the colony. He devoted much of his time to figuring out what the group would need in New England. He ordered all kinds of provisions like food, tools, and clothing. John also wrote an essay explaining why sincere Christians should consider moving to America. The first three reasons were to carry the gospel to the New World, to escape God's judgment that John believed was coming upon Europe, and to help solve the problems of overpopulation and poverty in England. John was worried that people in England were regarded as less valuable than horses and sheep.

As more people joined the company, it became clear that they needed a leader. They needed a man of faith and vision who could lead them to the New World. He had to be a man who could govern them once they arrived. Everyone thought that John was just that sort of man. He was very well respected for his fairness and wisdom. So in October, John was chosen as the first governor of the Massachusetts Bay Company.

Now that the company had ships, provisions, and a leader, they were ready to set sail. In mid-March of 1630, John said goodbye to Margaret and their children. Margaret was pregnant and John didn't think it would be safe for her or their younger children to travel yet. He wanted to bring over the rest of his family after the colony was better established. So John and Henry rode to Southampton to meet their ship, the *Arbella*.

A few days later, a fleet of 11 ships set sail—4 from Southampton, the other 7 from Bristol and Plymouth. Two days into the trip, the *Arbella* stopped at a port on the Isle of Wight. John had planned to set sail again within the week, but gusty winds and stormy seas delayed the *Arbella's* departure until April 8, 1630.

The entire fleet carried nearly 1,000 men, women, and children across the Atlantic Ocean. They brought along many supplies for the new colony. A cargo of goats, chickens, and pigs made the ships sound like noisy barns. They brought hammers, nails, and other carpenters' tools for building houses and churches. In addition to the wardrobe each person packed, an extra supply of cloth, shoes, and blankets were stocked for the whole colony. To defend themselves from attacks, the settlers carried armor, guns, and ammunition. Hoes, shovels, and other farming tools were brought for planting crops.

But they also needed to bring food to feed themselves now. The voyage would be long—

about two months across the Atlantic. Each family was supposed to be responsible for bringing their own supplies. Unfortunately, many people jumped on board at the last minute with little or no food. They had to beg for food from others who had little to spare.

Otherwise, the trip was calm. The *Arbella* sailed closely with three sister ships, which were usually in sight of each other. Children were able to run and play on deck. Their elders planned ahead and conducted worship services. Sometime during this period, John wrote his famous speech, "A Model of Christian Charity." In it, he described how he wanted the new settlement to be. "We shall be a city set on a hill," he predicted of the new colony, where the church would be the center of life. He described a Puritan community in which the government and church would work smoothly together. He argued for charity and decent human behavior. In New England, he wanted people to give up their selfish ways and work for the good of the colony.

On June 22, when they next saw land, it was the coastline of New England. Except for a few huts and clearings made by another group of settlers, there was nothing but forest. Some passengers decided not to stay when they saw this wilderness. They simply remained on the ships and sailed back to England. Most of the people aboard the *Arbella* went ashore to pick large, sweet wild strawberries. They welcomed the change from ship food, which was generally salty and cold. That night, John Endecott welcomed Winthrop and his staff. Two years earlier, Endecott had led a smaller group of settlers here. The men had a hearty meal of **venison,** corn, and beer.

The next day, John and many of the men began searching for a good location to build their homes. The women and children collected firewood. They needed to build fires to cook their meals. Initially, John chose the area known as Charlestown for their new colony. A house that could serve as the governor's headquarters had

After nearly three months at sea, John Winthrop and the other colonists saw land on June 22, 1630. They landed just north of where the Pilgrims, an earlier group of settlers, had landed in 1620.

already been built there. John and some of the men began building the governor's home nearby. Most of the other colonists put up wigwams, cloth tents, and other temporary shelters.

But some of the settlers couldn't help. They were still sick from the ocean voyage. Several had grown too weak from **malnutrition.** Sadly, within days of their arrival, quite a few people died. John suffered a personal tragedy. His son Henry had been strong and healthy, but he drowned in a river during their second week there. John was devastated but he had to be strong. He had a colony to govern.

Water was another problem. Massachusetts was bordered by a whole ocean of salt water, but the settlers really needed springs of fresh water. Because Charlestown was too far from any large springs, John decided they would have to find another area to live. Hearing of the colonists' problem, a clergyman named William Blackstone came to see John. Blackstone lived alone on the Shawmut peninsula across the river from Charlestown. He told John of the good spring there. The location also would be relatively safe from Indian attack. Blackstone invited the Puritans to join him there and they accepted. John had the frame of his house in Charlestown moved to the new site. On September 17, 1630, Governor Winthrop and his Court of Assistants named the site Boston.

Around the same time, the Puritans took a bold step. They had left England hoping to stay with the Church of England while cleansing it from within. But not long after arriving in the New World, they declared their religious independence. John, Thomas Dudley, Isaac Johnson, and John Wilson signed the Church Covenant. This united the New England Puritans in what became the First Church of Boston. In effect, they were now Separatists like the Pilgrims who had come over on the *Mayflower* 10 years earlier. Massachusetts Bay had also become the third colony, after Jamestown and Plymouth, in America.

The colonists' first winter in America was
very hard. Many died from disease and
starvation. When a ship from England
brought food just before all their supplies
ran out, John Winthrop proclaimed a day
of thanksgiving.

A Strong Leader

The Massachusetts Bay settlers had arrived too late in the season to plant and harvest any crops. For their first winter, they would have to rely on the provisions they brought over from England. Though they had planned for enough food, much of it had spoiled on the ships. And few of the settlers were prepared for the hardships of that first year. The climate was very different and the winter much colder than they had ever known. By November, John had lost 11 servants from his household. However, in letters to Margaret, he never mentioned despair.

Fall turned to winter. Out of nearly 1,000 settlers, 200 died that first winter—some from disease, others from starvation. By February, their food supplies almost ran out completely. But then a ship arrived, bringing new provisions. John distributed the food and proclaimed a day of thanksgiving to God. Things were never as bad again in Massachusetts. But the hardship persuaded many Puritans to stay home in England.

That spring, another 200 settlers gave up and went back to England. Many of the British investors decided that the colony was a losing business and took their money out. But John refused to give up. He invested large amounts of his own money to provide supplies for the colony. During that first full year, he almost single-handedly fed the colony out of his own pocket. John was confident that God was with the colony and would see them through, but he didn't just order others to do all the work. John rolled up his sleeves and helped to build shelters

Shipbuilding and the shipping trade soon became a major part of life in the early colony. Because wood was plentiful, ships could be built easily and cheaply.

along with everyone else. He led by example, and soon the whole company was working as hard as he.

Massachusetts Bay was steadily becoming a stable and productive colony. Shipyards started up in Boston and other ports along the Massachusetts coast. There were so many forests in

America that lumber was cheap. A ship cost about half as much to build in the colonies as it did in England. One of the first ships launched was the 30-ton *Blessing of the Bay*. It was dedicated to John. This was the first Massachusetts ship to trade with the Dutch in New Amsterdam (today's New York City). The ship carried fish, fur, horses, and wood to the West Indies where they were traded for molasses, indigo, and cotton. These goods were then sold in New Amsterdam for tobacco and furs, which were brought to England. In old England, the traders swapped these for manufactured goods, like furniture and tools, to bring back to New England.

A special shipment from England arrived for John in the fall of 1631. His beloved wife and the rest of his family finally came over to join him. Unfortunately, Margaret had to give John some bad news. Two more of their children had died in England. One was the newborn baby daughter whom he had never seen. John felt very sad.

Still, he thanked God for reuniting his family
with him.

John's oldest son was very happy to be in
New England. John Jr. was trained as a lawyer,
like his father, but he was also deeply interested
in both science and business. He looked for
ways to improve life in the colony. He saw that
the Puritans had to import many things from
England. One of the more expensive imports
was salt. Soon after arriving, John Jr. set up a
saltworks business. Thereafter, Massachusetts
could supply itself with all the salt it needed.

From the moment John joined the Massachusetts Bay Company, he kept a daily diary. Later
titled _The History of New England,_ John's diary
has become a valuable record of life in Massachusetts Bay. On the voyage across the Atlantic,
he had written about the weather and com-
plaints made by crew members and passengers.
Once in New England, he listed the arrivals of
ships and what they brought: more settlers,
more cattle, and more provisions. He wrote

Though the colonies had doctors, people often made their own remedies for common illnesses. One of John Winthrop's well-known recipes was oddly interesting. "Cut the sick man's nails and put the nails into a little bag of fine linen. Put a live eel into a tub of water. Tie the little bag of nails around the eel's neck. The eel will die, and the sick man will get better." It's doubtful that John's prescription actually cured any colds, but it probably scared many eels.

about fires and drownings. Puritans were superstitious and believed these were punishments made by God. In fact, storms, snakes, and illnesses were seen as signs from Satan or warnings from God.

Puritans felt that the law must be strictly obeyed if the community were to remain strong. Wrongdoers were punished for all types of crimes. In his diary, John mentioned executions and **banishments** of certain people. In June 1631, he noted the case of Philip Ratcliffe. John described the man as guilty of making "most foul, scandalous" remarks about the colony's church and government. That was a very serious crime in Puritan Massachusetts. John mentioned that Ratcliffe was "to be whipped, lose his ears, and be banished" from the colony. Sure enough, Ratcliffe wasn't seen again. Lesser crimes were punished by public humiliation. John wrote about a man named Robert Cole. It seems Cole was drunk on a regular basis. Puritans didn't prohibit drinking. In fact, most of them drank beer and hard cider with each meal. But they had rules against getting drunk. For his crime, Cole was sentenced to wear a large red letter "D" around his neck for a year.

Anyone found guilty of swearing, fighting, or other lighter crimes might be put in the stocks for a day. Stocks were made of wood and locked a person's arms and legs in place. Townspeople could yell insults, spit, or even throw things at the wrongdoer. These contraptions stood in the center of many Massachusetts towns. Ironically, the man who built the stocks in Boston was the first to occupy them. He was found guilty of overcharging for his services. These punishments seem harsh or odd today. But during the 1600s, they were not unusual in the colonies or in Europe.

To keep order in the colony, the Puritans used public humiliation as a method for punishing minor crimes. The guilty were secured in wooden stocks by their neck, arms, or legs in a public place where people could make jokes, call out insults, or throw things at them.

As Massachusetts grew, the Puritan leadership also had to deal with settlers who disagreed with their religious and political beliefs. These people were called **dissenters.** John and his followers had come to Massachusetts seeking freedom to practice their own religion. But in their colony, they didn't tolerate other religious beliefs. John had worked hard with the other leaders to allow only Puritans into the Massachusetts Bay Company. But early on, they were challenged by people with different views.

Roger Williams, a minister who had arrived in 1631, was one of the most troubling. Williams thought that the **magistrates** should have no voice in spiritual matters. He felt that their way forced religion on others. Williams also argued for Native Americans. He believed it was a sin to take Native American land without paying for it. In those days, the settlers generally thought native people were savages. They believed that the king owned the rights to the land. Therefore, the king could give away any of it to individuals or to groups. Some Europeans paid for the land they settled but that was rare. For his part, John had always encouraged the people of Massachusetts Bay to treat Native Americans with dignity and

Roger Williams arrived in Massachusetts Bay in 1631. Although he was also a Puritan, his beliefs were more liberal than those of the other colonists, and he was asked to leave the colony. He traveled south to establish another colony, Rhode Island.

respect. But he disagreed with Williams's other beliefs. By 1635, the leaders of the colony had heard enough from Williams. They had him arrested and ordered his return to England. But John was his friend and intervened. He suggested instead that Williams resettle in Rhode Island. Williams took John's wise advice.

Another dissenter was Anne Hutchinson. The 43-year-old mother of 14 was well-educated. She held meetings in her home to discuss Sunday sermons with other women. Hutchinson preached that obeying the laws of the colony was not that important for true Puritans.

Anne Hutchinson believed that God's laws were more important than man's laws. John Winthrop felt that this threatened authority in the colony. Anne was tried and banished; she too traveled south to live in Rhode Island.

She argued that God's grace held the saved above the law. John worried that her views threatened authority in the colony. The leaders called her an **antinomian,** because she spoke against the law. But it wasn't only her arguments that concerned the leaders. They also didn't like the fact that a woman was challenging their authority. They didn't think her actions were fitting for a female. And unlike Williams, she was drawing a lot of support. Most of that support came from merchants, with whom John had been having a lot of trouble. John had supported laws that controlled prices and profits because he wanted to limit selfish motives and give everyone in the community a chance to thrive. Merchants saw these laws simply as a threat to their business. But Hutchinson was soon silenced. Ministers tried to convert her to the Puritan way, but they were not successful. In 1637, she was tried before the magistrates. After two grueling days of questioning, Anne Hutchinson and her family were banished to Rhode Island.

In early Massachusetts, a threat to the church was a threat to the state. Anything that threatened it was evil and had to be stamped out. John saw both Williams and Hutchinson as threats, and his first concern was the peace of the community. John, the magistrates, and ministers did not hesitate to send other dissenters packing as well. They felt that was what it would take to keep their colony together.

Although the colony grew larger and thrived, none of the profits were being returned to England. The Puritans, determined to maintain their independence, formed a militia and placed cannons around Boston Harbor to defend the town against a possible English invasion.

4

A Colony Struggles and Thrives

Beyond crime and punishment, the growing colony faced other problems. The Massachusetts Bay Company had been started by and for Puritans. From the beginning, they decided that only church members could become **freemen**—or voting members. But most of the new settlers were not church members. And it wasn't easy to become a member. A person had to convert to Puritanism and provide proof of his or her sincere devotion. Usually, proof meant showing the church that a strong religious experience had convinced him or her of a new life in Christ. Ministers then decided whether or not that person was worthy of church membership. Because so many non-church members were joining the colony, Massachusetts Bay eventually allowed all property owners to have a vote, too.

It became clear that the Puritan leadership had to make a few other changes as well. The freemen confronted John about not following the original charter closely enough. They accused John and other magistrates of having too much power. The freemen demanded their full voting rights. Though John granted them all their chartered rights, the freemen still voted John out of the governor's office. In 1634, they elected Thomas Dudley as the new governor. But John was still widely respected by many. He continued to be the most influential man in the colony. Indeed, he served as deputy governor for many of the years he wasn't elected governor.

It wasn't only the freemen who felt that John and the other leaders had too much authority. The king of England was also concerned, but for different reasons. The English government thought that Massachusetts was becoming too independent. The colony had separated from the Church of England. Perhaps most troubling to Mother England was the loss of money. Massachusetts Bay had grown into a busy and profitable port of trade, but none of those profits were going back to England. The king soon demanded that Massachusetts return its charter.

John took charge of the situation. Massachusetts Bay was still legally owned by England but John would not submit to the king's demands. John ordered out the Massachusetts militia. He moved cannons around Boston Harbor to defend the town from possible British invasion. He had the **beacon** over Boston Common raised to warn of approaching naval ships. John did not want to start a war, but he would defend their settlement no matter what. The Puritans intended to maintain their independence—and they did.

Meanwhile, John had been working hard on getting schools set up in New England. The leaders of Massachusetts Bay were well educated and several of them read and spoke foreign languages. They valued learning and considered education a high priority. They wanted to make sure every child got a good education, partly so they could read and understand their Bibles. They also wanted to found a place of learning for ministers. In 1635, the Puritans opened the Boston Latin School, America's first public school. The next year, Boston families began contributing money to pay for a schoolmaster. Also in 1636, a college to train clergymen was established in New Towne (now Cambridge). A few years later, John Harvard gave the school his small fortune and personal library of about 300 books. Renamed after its generous donor, Harvard College became America's first college. John Winthrop, five other magistrates, and six ministers were named to Harvard's first Board of Overseers.

When John returned as governor in 1637, he was in financial trouble. His corrupt estate manager, James Luxford, had stolen money from

The Puritans valued education and wanted their children to be able to read the Bible. In 1635, they opened the Boston Latin School, America's first public school as noted in this sign at the original location on School Street in Boston.

John's estate. When the **fraud** was discovered, John owed a huge debt. He was forced to sell

As a strong leader, John Winthrop helped to improve the way of life for the people of Massachusetts. Consequently, Massachusetts led the early colonies in education, business, and public services. Here are some important firsts that took place during John's life:

- First Thanksgiving celebration
- First public park (Boston Common)
- First public secondary school (Boston Latin School)
- First college (Harvard)
- First printing press
- First post office
- First ironworks
- First public library

much of his property and borrow money. To help his father, John Jr. sold some of his land in Ipswich, Massachusetts. The colonists helped as well, by collecting voluntary donations. Because of all John had done for the community, he and Margaret were granted another estate of 3,000 acres. Luxford was tried, found guilty, and sentenced to have his ears chopped off. But John's problems didn't end there. Some felt that John should not be governor because he had "grown poor." In 1640, he was voted out of the governorship and did not return for two years.

At the same time, John had much to be

proud of. He was still widely respected for what he'd done for Massachusetts Bay. Ten years after its founding, the colony was thriving. Profitable shipments of herring, cod, furs, and lumber were being sold to England. Massachusetts was importing tools, provisions, furniture, and luxury items. Huts and one-room cottages were giving way to solid two-story homes with clapboard sides and shingled roofs. Wealthy families built large homes made of brick. The sounds of hammers and saws could be heard throughout Boston, Salem, and other port towns. More and more immigrants came. Some stayed in Boston. Others founded settlements of their own.

Massachusetts Bay granted land to groups of settlers for village sites. First to go up were meeting houses for church services and town meetings. The villages gave house lots to each family. The size of the lots depended on the size and rank of each family. Bigger lots went to larger, wealthier families. Just outside of town, land also was divided among farmers. A family might

In the early 1600s, silverware was a luxury enjoyed only by the wealthy. Depending on the meal, most people ate from a wooden bowl, using a spoon, their hands, maybe a knife—and plenty of napkins. The Winthrops, of course, were rich enough to have complete sets of spoons, knives, and forks all made from silver. On the *Arbella*, John was the only person to bring a silver fork. It was carefully placed in its own custom-made wooden case.

have a few acres around their home in town and 20 or 30 acres outside of town. Many farmers grazed their sheep and cows on the town common. They used oxen for plowing and planting the land in the country.

The population of Massachusetts was made up mainly of farming families. The Winthrops were among the wealthy minority. Inside the finer homes, there were tables, chairs, and bureaus made by skilled **artisans.** Some pieces were imported from England, while others were made in Boston. Many village houses only had rougher benches and tables. No houses had closets. They stored clothing and blankets in chests. The kitchen usually had a chest of drawers for pots and tableware. Many of the wealthy had silver. But most people ate from pewter dishes with spoons and their fingers. The rich hung curtains in their parlors and bedrooms and had chairs with leather or straw seats. Every home had a stone fireplace, typically 8 to 10 feet wide and hung with iron ladles and skillets. An oven in the chimney was used for baking beans and cornbread.

Despite their near starvation during the first winter, the colonists were now feeding themselves well. They had bacon, rabbit, and duck. In the early years, they didn't have enough cattle to kill for eating so they ate deer meat instead. Also easy to come by were wild turkey, geese, and pigeons. Lobster, shellfish, and all kinds of fish could be caught along the coast. Families grew most of their own vegetables and the herbs that were used in cooking and medicines. Lavender was often used for scenting linen. Their vegetable gardens might give them peas, beans, and cabbage as well as plenty of corn, which earlier settlers had learned how to grow and cook from

One of the oldest and best-known dishes the colonists made from corn was called Indian Pudding. This recipe is based on a Narragansett Indian dish.

Ingredients: 3 cups milk, $\frac{1}{3}$ cup molasses, $\frac{1}{3}$ cup cornmeal, 2 tablespoons butter, 1 beaten egg, 4 tablespoons of brown sugar, $\frac{1}{2}$ teaspoon cinnamon, $\frac{1}{2}$ teaspoon ground ginger, a pinch of salt.

Combine milk and molasses in a pan and stir over medium heat till blended. Stir in cornmeal. Stir until the mixture thickens. Blend in butter. Mix the other ingredients in a bowl. Gradually add the warm corn mixture into egg mixture and stir until blended. Bake in a 300°F oven for 80–90 minutes.

Native Americans. They ate it on the cob, in cornbread, and in pudding. One popular dish was hasty pudding, made with cornmeal mush and milk. And there was plenty of fruit, including apples and pears.

Puritans did not tolerate drunkenness, but they did enjoy their drink. Every family had a good store of wine, brandy, and sometimes whiskey. John and many of the ministers had small stills for making sweet liqueurs in their homes. Beer was considered as important as bread and many people had both at almost every meal.

Although many kitchen fireplaces had small ovens built into them for baking bread, almost all other cooking was done over an open fire. Pots were hung from iron hooks above the fire and meat or chicken was placed on a spit and roasted.

In the country, apple cider was the popular drink. Farmers would carry jugs of it out to the fields to refresh themselves while they worked.

A typical day for most farmers would start early in the morning. They would read the Bible

Before wool can be spun to make yarn for weaving or knitting, it must be combed, or carded, to remove leaves, sticks, and burrs that cling to it. The wool is pulled across a flat paddle with long, thin spikes in it. This makes the wool smooth, straight, and easier to spin.

before breakfast, which was usually **porridge** in wooden bowls. The men would then head out to the fields. The women would spend the morning cooking over log fires in the fireplace. At noon, they would sit down for dinner. This was the big meal of the day, when roast meats and succotash were heaped on pewter dishes. Succotash was a stew of meat, peas, corn, and other vegetables. Women often spent the afternoon cleaning and mending, while the men returned to the fields. At night, everyone would have cold meat, bread, and beer or cider. Children might get some hasty pudding. Bedtime was usually around eight o'clock because they had to rise early again the next morning.

Whether they were farmers, shopkeepers, or government leaders, all Puritans were hard workers. But they still found some time for play. Town meetings were considered a night out. Everyone looked forward to church on Sunday morning and afternoon, as no work was allowed. And for one or two days every month, each town had militia training. Entire families would come with picnics to watch their men run through drills on the town common. At the end of harvest season, whole towns might get together again to celebrate their bounty.

In 1636, a college for the training of clergymen was formed across the Charles River from Boston. A few years later, John Harvard gave the school his money and personal library, which prompted the trustees to rename the school Harvard College.

A Growing
Colony

From 1630 to 1640, a period called the **Great Migration** brought more than 20,000 people to New England. Despite the initial purpose of the Massachusetts Bay Company—to establish a Puritan colony—only a few of these thousands were Puritans. Many **emigrants** made the journey simply for economic or political reasons. They were attracted by the free land and by the opportunities for trade. They wanted to get rich and improve their social status. They came, in other words, for personal gain—precisely what John had worked so hard to avoid.

One of the first writers to offer a glimpse into everyday colonial life was Anne Bradstreet. When she was 18 years old, the poet made the long journey from Southampton, England, to Massachusetts Bay. She and her husband, Simon, were aboard the *Arbella* with John Winthrop. The wife of a magistrate and mother of eight children, Anne had much to keep her busy. Somehow, she still found time to write poetry. Nearly 20 years after arriving, Anne Bradstreet published the first poetry book written in the 13 colonies. It was titled *The Tenth Muse, Lately Sprung Up in America.*

By 1640, as the number and size of towns were increasing, more schoolhouses went up. The students were likely to study books their families brought over, as well as newer volumes imported from England. But a man named Stephen Daye wanted to start printing titles in America. In the cellar of the president's house at Harvard College, he set up the first printing press in America. Daye hired some bookbinders and, in 1640, printed the *Bay Psalm Book.* It was the first English-language book published in America. The book was a collection of biblical psalms translated from Hebrew by some of the colony's leading clergymen.

Of all the imports from England, iron was one of the more costly. And the colonies still had to import most of their iron goods. Given enough iron, the town blacksmith might make horseshoes, pots, nails, weapons, and plows. That meant everyone from housewives to farmers to gentlemen used something made from the mineral. When a lot of bog iron was found in nearby ponds, John Jr. had an idea. He told his father he wanted to start an ironworks in Massachusetts. They agreed that it was necessary. But it would cost a lot of money. In 1641, John Jr. headed back to England to raise the money.

A charming and persuasive man, John Jr. convinced many wealthy men to invest their money. He returned to Massachusetts two years later with tools and materials for the ironworks. He also brought back some skilled workmen. These workmen were welcomed for their expertise but they weren't Puritans. They did not easily fit in at first. Several of them appeared in court, charged with drunkenness and absence from church. Many more were found guilty of violating sumptuary laws–the laws that regulated who could wear what types of clothing. Such laws separated the upper class from the lower classes and forbade wearing work clothes to church.

Laborers wore leather and canvas or other coarse fabrics. Upper- and middle-class men wore suits of **doublets,** vests, and **breeches.** The wealthier a person was, the more color and flash they could get away with. Some men wore coats trimmed with silver lace. Many wore bright vests and colorful cloaks with silver buttons. During the mid-17th century, few people wore black, except for formal occasions. Under their vests and jackets, men wore white or dyed long-sleeved linen shirts. Some men wore blue silk garters over their leggings just below the knee.

Women dressed in bright colors, too. They wore full, ankle-length skirts, tight bodices, and caps. For special occasions, the wealthy had gowns made of silk or other fine fabrics. If they wore jewelry, it was usually something simple, like gold or silver rings. Many women wore tortoiseshell combs in their hair. They might wear cloaks with silk hoods, shawls, and scarves. Some of the fabrics were imported. But the colonists also raised flax to spin and weave into linen. They raised sheep for wool. To get the bright colors they loved, they dyed their own fabrics. For blue shades, indigo was imported from Barbados. Hickory and oak bark were used for brown dyes. Purple came from iris petals and orange from sassafras.

However, John Winthrop considered safety far more important than the colony's fashion. As the colony grew and put down deeper roots, it needed greater protection. More settlers meant more fighting over land with Native Americans. There was also the risk of attack from England. Since early on, every male between 15 and 60 years old had been part of the militia. They had to appear for training once a month. Each man had to provide his own gun and ammunition. Most men molded their own lead bullets. With more colonies being founded, John saw a need for military cooperation. He knew there would be greater strength in numbers, so he urged towns in surrounding colonies to band together. He felt that this was the only way they could ensure everyone's safety. In 1643, the colonies formed the New England Confederation. Massachusetts was the largest member, with 15,000 people. The other colonies had about 2,000 people each.

Throughout his life in Massachusetts, John sacrificed many of his personal needs for the greater good of the colony. Asking for sacrifices from all the colonists, he settled for no less from himself. For many years, John went without a salary. When the colony could not pay for something, he spent his own money for public purposes. Oddly, in 1645, his generosity created some enemies. Some officials, including the deputy governor, criticized the way he

As more colonists settled in the area
around Boston and took more land to farm,
they came into conflict with the Native
Americans in the area and had to defend
themselves. Every male between the ages
of 15 and 60 was a member of the militia
and trained once a month.

Cotton Mather was a respected Puritan minister and historian in colonial times. His most famous work, *Magnalia Christi Americana*, gives an example of John Winthrop's generosity. During a long, hard winter when wood was scarce, one of John's needy neighbors stole wood from his pile. The governor responded, angrily, "Does he so; I'll take a course with him; go call that man to me; I'll warrant you I'll cure him of stealing." When the man came, Winthrop said to him, "Friend, it is a severe winter, and I doubt you are but meanly provided for wood; wherefore I would have you supply yourself at my woodpile till the cold season be over."

managed the colony. A committee of clergy declared that John had been too generous in handing down decisions and ordering punishments. They felt John hadn't been tough enough. At the same time, some junior government deputies complained that they didn't have enough power. They took the opportunity to verbally attack him. John answered all the charges publicly but the deputies still demanded to hear his case in full. He was called before the General Court, where he argued his case over the course of seven weeks. In the end, the General Court completely cleared John of all charges and fined his accusers.

John served as the governor of Massachusetts on and off between 1630 and 1648. He had led Massachusetts Bay from a struggling settlement to a modern, thriving capital. Boston had bakers, weavers, felt makers, brick and tile makers, leather workers, and carpenters.

In 1647, John passed one of the most important laws in American history. It ordered towns of 50 or more families to have a school that was partly paid for by taxes. This marked the start of America's public-school system. Also during his last term, John had to deal with one more in a long line of religious and political dissenters. Robert Child warned that he would ask England's Parliament to reduce the colony's independence. Child was promptly fined for contempt and John declared that Massachusetts Bay did not answer to England. In other words, Massachusetts was no longer a colony, but a self-sufficient community.

Over in England, a Puritan revolution had been gaining momentum. A number of Puritans felt torn between building their new life in America and returning to help their friends in England. Some of John's friends urged him to return to help the cause. But John felt that it was his duty to stay in Massachusetts, where he and his followers had already risked so much for their religious freedom. He supported his Puritan friends in England but continued to focus his efforts on building Massachusetts. As it turned out, the Puritans seized control of England within a few years anyway.

In the summer of 1647, John endured one of the greatest personal tragedies of his life. After 30 years together, he lost his beloved Margaret. During their marriage, they had reared four children. (Margaret had given birth to eight children, but four died at birth.) Indeed, at the time of Margaret's death, John had seven grown children. Not one to dwell on his grief, John turned all his attention to governing Massachusetts.

Nearly one year later in 1648, he married for the fourth and last time. Martha Coytmore, his new wife, was soon expecting a child. John barely lived to see his last son born. On March 26, 1649, John died at home in Boston. He was 61 years old.

John Winthrop served as governor of the colony for many years. He established many important features of the new colony. He mandated public schools, established the New England Confederation to help defend the colony, and worked to improve the lives of all the colonists.

Puritans generally disapproved of excessive mourning or elaborate funerals. But John's funeral was honored as a public holiday to celebrate his accomplishments. With unusual fanfare, the Massachusetts artillery set off a barrel and a half of gun powder in a series of musket shots. Everyone came together to honor Massachusetts's first great citizen.

During his life, John suffered through loved ones' deaths, political disputes, financial losses, and more. He also enjoyed many rewards for his hard work and strong faith. Through it all, he sacrificed so much for the good of others. John was a great leader. He managed to hold Massachusetts Bay together through its early hardships and never stopped striving to make life in the colony better for everyone. A hard-working and generous man, he led by example. John was a wise, fair, and dedicated Puritan leader. Though the nature of Massachusetts Bay Colony changed over time, John's ideals and hopes left their mark. Perhaps, more than anyone else, he gave the colony its distinctive character.

GLOSSARY

antinomian Greek word meaning anti-law

artisans craftsmen

banishment to be expelled to another state or country

beacon warning light

breeches knee-length pants worn by men

dissenter someone who disagrees with church beliefs

doublets close-fitting jackets worn by men

dowry money and/or property a woman brings to her marriage

emigrant person who moves from his or her native country to settle in another land

fraud deception, typically involving the stealing of money

freemen voting members of the church

Great Migration period between 1630 and 1640, when 20,000 people landed in Massachusetts Bay

justice of the peace person selected by a community to settle disputes and perform marriages and other services

magistrates government officials

malnutrition illness caused by not eating enough healthy food

Parliament England's lawmaking body

porridge a soft food made from boiling grains such as oatmeal in milk

Puritans group of Protestants who broke from the Church of England to worship in their own way

CHRONOLOGY

1588 John Winthrop is born in Edwardstone, England, on January 22.

1602 Attends Trinity College for 18 months.

1605 Marries Mary Forth.

1615 Mary Forth Winthrop dies; John marries Thomasine Clopton.

1616 Thomasine Clopton Winthrop dies.

1617 Made justice of the peace in Suffolk County, England.

1618 Marries Margaret Tyndal.

1627 Becomes an attorney at Court of Wards and Liveries, London.

1629 Joins the Massachusetts Bay Company; elected governor, serves three one-year terms.

1630 Emigrates to Massachusetts.

1637 Reelected governor, serves two terms; suffers huge financial loss.

1642 Reelected governor for one term.

1643 Organizes New England Confederation agreement among colonies.

1646 Reelected governor and serves two terms.

1647 Margaret Tyndal Winthrop dies.

1648 Marries Martha Coytmore.

1649 John Winthrop dies at his home in Boston on March 26.

COLONIAL TIME LINE

1607 Jamestown, Virginia, is settled by the English.

1620 Pilgrims on the *Mayflower* land at Plymouth, Massachusetts.

1623 The Dutch settle New Netherlands, the colony that later becomes New York.

1630 Massachusetts Bay Colony is started.

1634 Maryland is settled as a Roman Catholic colony. Later Maryland becomes a safe place for people with different religious beliefs.

1636 Roger Williams is thrown out of the Massachusetts Bay Colony. He settles Rhode Island, the first colony to give people freedom of religion.

1682 William Penn forms the colony of Pennsylvania.

1688 Pennsylvania Quakers make the first formal protest against slavery.

1692 Trials for witchcraft are held in Salem, Massachusetts.

1712 Slaves revolt in New York. Twenty-one blacks are killed as punishment.

1720 Major smallpox outbreak occurs in Boston. Cotton Mather and some doctors try a new treatment. Many people think the new treatment shouldn't be used.

1754 French and Indian War begins. It ends nine years later.

1761 Benjamin Banneker builds a wooden clock that keeps precise time.

1765 Britain passes the Stamp Act. Violent protests break out in the colonies. The Stamp Act is ended the next year.

1775 The battles of Lexington and Concord begin the American Revolution.

1776 Declaration of Independence is signed.

FURTHER READING

Dickinson, Alice. *The Colony of Massachusetts*. New York: Franklin Watts, 1975.

Earle, A.M. *Child Life in Colonial Days*. Williamstown, MA: Corner House Publishers, 1989.

Egger-Bovet, H., and M. Smith-Baranzini. *Brown Paper School USKids History: Book of the American Colonies*. Boston: Little, Brown, 1996.

Ichord, L. F. *Hasty Pudding, Johnnycakes, and Other Good Stuff: Cooking in Colonial America*. Brookfield, CT: Millbrook Press, 1998.

McGovern, Ann. . . . *If You Lived in Colonial Times*. New York: Scholastic, 1992.

McNair, S. *Massachusetts*. Danbury, CT: Children's Press, 1998.

INDEX

INDEX

PICTURE CREDITS

ABOUT THE AUTHOR

As director of Write Stuff Editorial Services in New York City, **ELIZABETH RUSSELL CONNELLY** has written and edited for medical and business journals, trade magazines, high-tech firms, and various book publishers. She earned an MBA from New York University's Stern School in 1993 and a certificate in language studies from Freiburg Universitaet (Switzerland) in 1985. Her published work includes a global studies book for young adults, more than 14 Access travel guides covering North America, the Caribbean, and Europe, and several volumes in Chelsea House Publishers' series ENCYCLOPEDIA OF PSYCHOLOGICAL DISORDERS.

Senior Consulting Editor **ARTHUR M. SCHLESINGER, JR.** is the leading American historian of our time. He won the Pulitzer Prize for his book *The Age of Jackson* (1945) and again for *A Thousand Days* (1965). This chronicle of the Kennedy Administration also won a National Book Award. He has written many other books including a multi-volume series, *The Age of Roosevelt.* Professor Schlesinger is the Albert Schweitzer Professor of the Humanities at the City University of New York, and has been involved in several other Chelsea House projects, including the REVOLUTIONARY WAR LEADERS biographies on the most prominent figures of early American history.